ACTIVITY BANK

Coping with Change

Tina Rae

Contents

Editor: Terry Vittachi
Layout artist: Patricia Hollingsworth
Illustrations: Bob Farley – Graham-Cameron Illustration (p23) and Charmaine Peters

© 2000 Folens Limited, on behalf of the author.

Every effort has been made to contact copyright holders of material used in this book. If any have been overlooked, we will be pleased to make any necessary arrangements.

First published 2000 by Folens Limited, Dunstable and Dublin.
Reprinted 2000.

Folens Limited, Albert House, Apex Business Centre, Boscombe Road, Dunstable, LU5 4RL, England.

ISBN 1 86202 563–0

How to use this book

There are 22 activities contained within this book. Each one has a teacher instruction page and a pupil activity page. The activities can be completed in short time slots or extended into longer periods, depending on the length of time you have available. They can also be differentiated to suit the needs of less able pupils. The activities can be presented in any order and you do not have to work your way right through the book. A matrix on page 48 provides a useful summary of, and reference to, the skills that pupils will learn through each activity, but we do recommend that Activity 1 and Activity 2 are presented at the beginning of the series of lessons and Activity 22 as a review at the end.

Most of the activities in this book need few materials or resources other than copies of the activity sheet, paper and pens. They are designed to keep the teacher's workload to a minimum beyond planning how each activity will be carried out in the classroom. Most are designed so that pupils can work individually, in pairs or in small groups, depending on the teacher's preference. We recommend a balance of whole class, small group and individual work to provide pupils with plenty of opportunity to express their views, to listen to and try to understand the views of others and to develop communication and social skills. Teachers will also need to be aware of the sensitivities of the pupils' cultural and religious backgrounds when planning their lessons.

The aims and expected outcomes of each activity are clearly indicated and the format for all activities is consistent to enable you quickly to feel comfortable and familiar with the style. All the information a teacher needs is contained here, not only to present the lesson confidently, but also to answer most questions that arise.

Introduction

Possibly the greatest changes experienced by most pupils occur during the first few years at secondary school. They are moved from smaller and generally more intimate environments into larger institutions with numerous new rules and systems. Alongside coping with this change, they also have to deal with the often confusing physical and emotional changes that occur during puberty. Family contexts and support systems available to pupils will vary considerably, as will pupils' responses to these changes. However, what is clearly needed for all pupils is the opportunity to confront, discuss, accept, understand and deal with these changes in a safe and constructive environment. Such changes can very easily affect both academic progress and emotional development.

Schools, as institutions, have a clear focus and required commitment to teaching a curriculum and basic skills – in other words, the three Rs. It is evident, however, that without a further commitment to teaching the 'fourth R' or 'life skills' such as problem solving, empathy, cooperation, social skills and emotional literacy, schools will be failing many pupils. Without these skills and the sense of personal identity, self-esteem and self-control that can result from focusing upon them, some pupils will not develop academically or emotionally to their full potential.

This Activity Bank title, *Coping with Change*, aims to provide resources for the PSHE curriculum, helping to meet both the requirements of OFSTED regarding moral and social guidance and the DfEE's Framework for PSHE. This will support pupils in coping with changes and developments occurring at this time and in developing the necessary life skills to manage and maintain the transition to secondary school and beyond.

A big move

The changes I shall encounter at secondary school

AIMS

To highlight the changes that pupils might have to cope with at secondary school and to identify both the myths and realities surrounding those changes.

Teaching Points

◆ The move from primary to secondary school is possibly the biggest change that most pupils face in their school career. It can cause confusion and anxiety.
◆ Pupils need adequate support structures in order to enable them to cope with this change.
◆ The aim of this lesson is to make pupils aware that they can gain much support from within the peer group itself.

USING THE ACTIVITY SHEET

The focus of the activity is to explore reactions to change and to clarify for pupils both the myths and realities of the changes they are currently experiencing.

Step 1 Ask the class the following questions: What were you looking forward to at secondary school? What were the main differences you found between primary school and secondary school? What were you most concerned about? Write the pupils' responses on the board. Ask the pupils to complete the first question on the activity sheet.

Step 2 Split the class into small groups and ask them to discuss the list of concerns on the board and to make a note of any that they decide were unfounded.

Step 3 Ask each group to nominate one person to feed back responses to the rest of the class. Put a line through the concerns listed on the board that the class agree were unfounded. Highlight similarities and differences in the responses.

Step 4 Ask the pupils to complete the second and third questions on the activity sheet to identify problems that pupils might face at a new school and how these might be solved.

Extension Activities

◆ Ask pupils to write an interview between a new pupil and a pupil who is already at the school. Ask them to consider the many questions that the new pupil might ask.
◆ The pupils could contribute to a picture-story cartoon booklet in which they describe fears or worries that turned out to be unfounded. This could be published and distributed to new pupils before they arrive at the school.

Outcomes

◆ Understanding a distinction between fact and fiction.
◆ An understanding that to express a fear and accept help is not a sign of weakness.
◆ Developing empathy for each other through the recognition of shared fears, beliefs and needs.

A big move

1. Complete the diary of your first day at a new school.

What I did	How I felt
9am _____	_____
10am _____	_____
11am _____	_____
12pm _____	_____
1pm _____	_____
2pm _____	_____
3pm _____	_____
4pm _____	_____

2. List six events that might cause problems for a pupil on the first day at a new school.

1. _____
2. _____
3. _____
4. _____
5. _____
6. _____

3. How would you solve the problems?

1. _____
2. _____
3. _____
4. _____
5. _____
6. _____

Helping yourself

Things I can do to make change easier

AIMS

To highlight how students can develop their own range of self-help strategies in order to cope with the change brought about by secondary school transfer.

Teaching Points

◆ After pupils have spent two or three days in their new secondary schools they begin to absorb the daily routines and structures and become aware of a much faster pace of life.
◆ Adults within the school context make provision for new pupils to integrate into the systems as swiftly and as comfortably as possible.
◆ Older siblings and members of pupils' own peer group at school may provide support and reassurance.
◆ All pupils will benefit from developing their own practical strategies and skills to cope with change, such as developing a bank of self-help plans and ideas.
◆ Provide pupils with information as to where they might go to get help, for example prefects, form teachers.
◆ An induction self-help programme could include a 'who's who' form for pupils to fill in. This could make use of any internal school documents.

USING THE ACTIVITY SHEET

The focus of the activity is to reinforce the ways in which students can develop their own personal range of strategies to cope with change.

Step 1 Ask pupils, in pairs, to discuss the following questions and write the responses on the board: What are the main differences between secondary school and primary school? Which of these do you think would cause the greatest problem for a new pupil? What help is available for new pupils in the school? Where can they get help? Reinforce the support that is currently available in school for new pupils.

Step 2 Split the class into small groups. Ask each group to list at least ten problems that a new pupil might face on the first day at school,

such as 'You can't find your way around the building.' Make two column headings on the board entitled 'problem' and 'solution'. Ask each group to swap problems with another group who have to write a solution. Encourage solutions that develop self-help strategies. Invite the groups to read out their problems and solutions.

Step 3 Ask pupils to complete the activity sheet. This involves formulating a list of 'helpful hints'. Pupils may wish to work in pairs or small groups in order to share ideas.

Extension Activities

◆ Invite pupils to write an account or draw a strip cartoon entitled 'A day in the life of a secondary school pupil' and send it to their Year 6 teacher who can read it to his or her present class.
◆ Ask pupils to compile an information booklet that gives advice to new pupils on how to cope with the transfer to the next year. You could involve the English and the ICT Departments.

Outcomes

◆ An ability to distinguish between strategies that rely on others and those that rely more on ourselves, and to recognise that we all need to make use of both kinds of strategies.
◆ Recognising that every individual is capable, to varying degrees, of developing self-help skills and strategies – we can all help ourselves and each other.

Helping yourself

Think of some helpful hints for a new pupil at your school. Write the problem in the thought bubble and the solution in the box.

This will help you.

Working it out

The external and internal influences on my behaviour

AIMS

To highlight the ways in which pupils' responsibilities will change and develop at secondary school.

Teaching Points

◆ For many pupils, the transfer to secondary school will involve taking on new responsibilities. The most important one will probably be assuming more responsibility for themselves and their time.

◆ Making these kinds of changes can be difficult for some pupils, whereas those who feel self-confident and have good self-esteem may find the adjustment easier.

◆ A significant part of growing up involves taking on more responsibility for oneself and for others. The pace of this may be influenced by a variety of factors such as differences in culture, gender and economic background, and these issues will need to be sensitively handled.

USING THE ACTIVITY SHEET

The focus of the activity is to explore how pupils' responsibilities will necessarily change at secondary school and how this may affect both self-esteem and confidence.

Step 1   Ask pupils to list the responsibilities they had at primary school, both at home and at school. Ask them to list the responsibilities they have now. Then ask them to decide whether or not they have more responsibilities now. Initiate a class discussion on this topic, focusing on the differences between primary and secondary school responsibilities.

Step 2   Ask the pupils to consider ways in which to ensure that they meet their new responsibilities. What difficulties might there be (such as time management)?

Step 3   Ask each group to present their work to the rest of the class. Highlight the similarities and differences in their responses.

Step 4   Ask the pupils to complete the activity sheet. Encourage them to think particularly about how their responsibilities have changed.

Extension Activities

◆ The pupils could make lists of the things they have to do and decide how they know which to do first. (They need to consider deadlines for things such as homework and having things such as their PE or swimming kit ready; they also need to consider the relative importance of each item on the list.) They could give each item on the list a priority A, B or C.

◆ Give the class the following scenario: Mark has been in trouble every day for forgetting his homework or not completing it. Ask pupils what advice they would give him. They could write him a letter in pairs.

Outcomes

◆ An understanding that new responsibilities need not cause problems if they are dealt with systematically.

◆ Recognising that we can use various strategies to help us to become more organised and efficient.

◆ Developing cooperation and problem-solving skills with regard to new responsibilities.

Working it out

You have two small children living next door. Your younger brother frequently goes to play with them and vice versa. The problem is, now that you are at secondary school, you have homework to do every evening. The younger children make so much noise that you can't concentrate and your little brother doesn't understand why you don't have time to play with him as you used to. What can you do? Try to work it out by answering the questions below.

1. State the problem: _____

_____

_____

2. Think of as many solutions as you can (at least three!).

_____

_____

_____

3. Think ahead to the consequences – 'What will happen if...?'

_____

_____

_____

4. Choose your best plan. What is it? Why did you choose it?

_____

_____

_____

How should I behave?

Understanding the differences between right and wrong

— AIMS —

To highlight the need for everyone to become morally aware in order to play a positive role both at school and at home.

Teaching Points

Materials needed
Prepare a set of cards for pupils to write on.

◆ By the time pupils reach secondary school they generally have some understanding of what constitutes acceptable and unacceptable behaviour in the world around them.
◆ There will be general agreement regarding the breakdown of order should people steal, murder, commit acts of arson and so on. There may be disagreement regarding other issues, such as the role of women, homosexual relationships, racism and drugs.
◆ Pupils should regard making moral choices as a personal responsibility.

— USING THE ACTIVITY SHEET —

The focus of the activity is to explore the need to adhere to moral precepts in order to enable everyone to feel secure and safe in their environment.

Step 1   Ask the pupils to contribute to a list of things they think people should not do. Collate their ideas on the board. Ask them, in groups, to copy each item on to a separate card.

Step 2   In their groups, the pupils share out the cards. They take turns to put a card on the table, first placing the actions that are the most severe at one end of the table and following them with those that are less severe at the other end. As they place a card on the table they should justify its position (by comparing its severity with the other actions). Each member of the group then has an opportunity to move a card to a different place, explaining this move.

Step 3   Compare the ways in which the groups have arranged the actions. What does the class think are the worst things people can do?

Step 4   Ask pupils to complete the activity sheet. In a plenary session, discuss pupils' responses to the questions it poses and highlight similarities and differences.

Step 5   Ask each group to think of a dilemma and use this as a starting point for class discussion. Highlight how part of the process of growing up involves making 'moral' decisions and working out personal belief systems that we can justify and feel comfortable with.

Extension Activities

◆ Invite pupils to design a poster warning each other about the dangers of one of the following: cheating, lying or disobedience.
◆ Ask pupils to devise their own ten rules of behaviour – what should people do and what should they not do? Each rule could be phrased: 'You should ...' or 'You should not ...'.

Outcomes

◆ Learning to distinguish between 'right' and 'wrong' actions and recognising the need for rules and laws to regulate behaviour.
◆ Recognising the importance of being a responsible individual who has the ability and duty to make moral judgements and choices.

How should I behave?

Read the story.

1. Everyone in the class has new trainers except Joe.

2. He is called names on the way home and feels angry because his mum can't afford to buy new trainers this month.

3. At home he sees his mum's purse in the kitchen.

4. He decides to take the money saved for the gas bill out of the purse and run out of the house.

Now imagine you are Joe

1. Why do you feel angry with your classmates and your mum?

_____

2. Were your classmates 'right' to make their comments to you? If not, why not?

_____

3. Why can't you wait until your mum could afford new trainers?

_____

4. Do you think you have done something wrong?

_____

5. What do you think will happen next?

_____

6. How could you sort out this problem you have made for yourself?

_____

Saying 'no'

Making the right choices

AIMS

To highlight situations in which pupils need to be able to say 'no' in order to remain safe or to maintain their self-esteem.

Teaching Points

◆ In addition to taking on more responsibility for themselves and their actions, secondary school pupils will be exposed to new and significant pressures and choices.

◆ Pupils will need to be very certain of their belief systems, particularly ideas about what is 'right' and 'wrong', to resolve the dilemmas they face as peer pressure to conform increases.

◆ Pupils will need to develop social and moral skills that allow them to assert their views, enabling them to say 'no' when pressurised to take part in certain activities.

USING THE ACTIVITY SHEET

The focus of the activity is to explore when to say 'no' and provide pupils with practice in doing so.

Step 1   Ask the class the following questions and collate the answers on the board: In what kind of situations should you say 'No, I don't want to do that'? Can you explain why you should say 'no'? Where can you get support in these situations?

Step 2   Split the class into groups and ask them to list four scenarios in which they have to be assertive and say 'no', such as: 'My friend said he would stop talking to me if I didn't help him steal from the music shop.' Response: be firm and honest, say that you don't feel happy stealing and would rather he didn't. Ask groups to swap their lists and discuss and write down ways to say 'no' for each scenario.

Step 3   Ask each group to feed back one problem and solution to the class. Highlight the similarities between the problems and the importance of being able to say 'no' and of having reasoned arguments for doing so. Emphasise that everyone has a right to refuse to become involved in things that he or she feels are wrong, or that make them feel uncomfortable.

Step 4   Ask pupils to consider the situations depicted on the activity sheet, to decide on the best advice for each person and then to express it in one ot two 'priority' sentences. It might be useful to discuss the ways in which pupils can use humour to be assertive without appearing to be 'goody-goody'.

Extension Activities

◆ Ask pupils to write a short scene between two characters where one pupil is trying to persuade the other to go to a drug-taking party. The other pupil does not want to go and needs to say 'no'. Invite them to act out the scene with a friend.

◆ Suggest that everyone writes an illustrated poem entitled 'Saying no'. They should try to include everything that they have a right to say 'no' to, such as stealing, cheating and vandalism, and explain why.

Outcomes

◆ Awareness of situations in which pupils need to be able to say no, particularly those involving substance abuse, smoking and under-age sex, and how to deal with them.

◆ Knowledge of the dangers of substance abuse, smoking and under-age sex.

◆ An understanding of the basic 'right' to self-protection and adult support against emotional and physical abuse of all kinds.

Saying 'no'

How can Helen, Ranjit and Greg say 'no'? Think carefully. Make notes about the advice you would give them. Write your advice on the cards in one or two sentences.

Helen

'My friend's older brother hands out some ecstasy tablets at a party. I don't want to take one.'

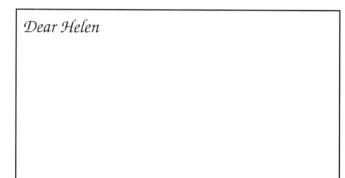

Dear Helen

Ranjit

'My friend says I should smoke because it makes you look cool and older, especially at parties.'

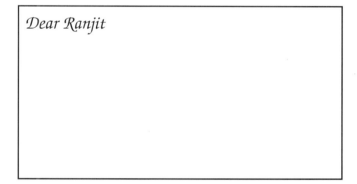

Dear Ranjit

Greg

'My girlfriend wants me to buy her a ring. I haven't got the money, but she says if I don't get her one she'll finish with me.'

Dear Greg

Thinking about others

Seeing things from other people's point of view

AIMS

To highlight the need for pupils to develop empathy with others within their peer group and to recognise how they can help others to feel accepted and secure.

Teaching Points

◆ At secondary school, pupils will face an increased need to 'fit in' and conform.

◆ It is important to ensure that pupils learn to recognise and accept 'difference' and to take responsibility for their own actions, views and beliefs.

◆ This session will provide an opportunity to highlight and also to celebrate differences within the group and to reinforce how pupils can support one another even if their belief systems are entirely different.

◆ It will highlight how racial, sexual and religious prejudice affects pupils and their families, and will encourage pupils to formulate their own views and responses to these issues.

USING THE ACTIVITY SHEET

The focus of the activity is to explore the notion of 'difference' and encourage pupils to consider what kinds of changes they would need to make if they were to swap places with someone else.

Step 1   Ask pupils to complete the activity sheet.

Step 2   Draw two columns on the board, headed 'differences' and 'similarities'. Ask the class to think of words to describe our similarities and differences and write them on the board. Deal with racial, gender and religious differences sensitively.

Step 3   Split the class into pairs. Ask each pair to list five situations in which a pupil may be teased or bullied for being 'different'. Then ask each group to devise a 'support plan' for these pupils. Give an example: Cara is being teased and bullied because she is a black African girl and has a different accent. Support plan: tell the bullies to stop and leave her alone, report the bullies to teachers, be a friend to Cara, ask Cara about her culture and her beliefs and so on.

Step 4   Ask pupils to choose one situation to act out to the rest of the class. Use this as a starting point for discussion, highlighting ways in which pupils can support each other and allow for and respect differences.

Extension Activities

◆ Put together a series of cards depicting different situations to be used in class (e.g. being bullied for not wearing the right fashion, liking classical music, physical appearance). Pupils can be asked what they might do in each situation and the possible consequences.

◆ Ask pupils to design a poster to reinforce the slogan 'It's good to be different' or to reinforce an anti-racist or anti-sexist message such as 'Change your attitude – don't be racist or sexist.'.

Outcomes

◆ Increased awareness of difference and the need to accept, value and respect this within the peer group.

◆ Increased responsibility towards others by recognising the need to change inappropriate behaviour and attitudes amongst friends and members of the peer group.

◆ An awareness of support systems available to those at risk of bullying.

Thinking about others

Describe an imaginary person. Give him or her a name. Draw a picture.

Now describe someone else who is entirely different. If the other person was male, describe a female and so on.

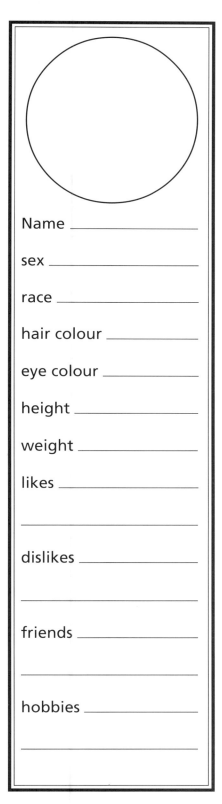

Name _____

sex _____

race _____

hair colour _____

eye colour _____

height _____

weight _____

likes _____

_____

dislikes _____

_____

friends _____

_____

hobbies _____

_____

Now answer these questions:

1. Which of these people would you prefer to be? Why?

_____

_____

_____

2. How would life be different if you were the other person?

_____

_____

_____

3. How would people treat you? Better? Worse? Just the same? Why?

_____

_____

_____

4. Would your life be better? Worse? Just the same? Why?

_____

_____

_____

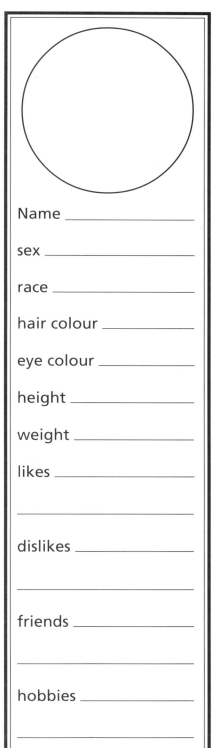

Name _____

sex _____

race _____

hair colour _____

eye colour _____

height _____

weight _____

likes _____

_____

dislikes _____

_____

friends _____

_____

hobbies _____

_____

Friends for life?

How to cope with changing relationships

AIMS

To highlight how relationships and friendships change through time and our need to adapt to meet such changes.

Teaching Points

◆ During their time at secondary school, many pupils will experience change in terms of the make-up of their peer group.
◆ Many pupils might feel somewhat apprehensive regarding the nature and status of existing friendships and perhaps concerned about making new friends and the impact this may have on their established relationships.
◆ For those pupils who do not have an established support system of friends, changes in peer group can add pressure to an already disruptive time.
◆ Although such changes in relationships and friendships can be difficult to cope with, it is important to emphasise the kind of support that pupils can offer each other and the shared nature of such experiences.

USING THE ACTIVITY SHEET

The focus of the activity is to explore and reinforce notions of friendship and the social skills needed to form such friendships.

Step 1   Ask pupils to complete the activity sheet. They can work individually or in pairs and then compare ideas.

Step 2   Ask the whole class to share their ideas about what friends do for each other. Collate their answers on the board.

Step 3   Ask the pupils to brainstorm, in groups, ways of making friends and then write down some 'rules' on: 'how to make friends', 'how to keep your friends' or even 'how to lose friends'.

Step 4   The pupils could share their ideas from Step 3. Ask them what strategies they have developed to make and keep friends.

Extension Activities

◆ 'Ring' activities could be used to accelerate new friendships and promote group feelings. For example, a facial expression could be sent around a circle, or make a circle linking hands and ask one person to try 'breaking in' or 'breaking out' of the circle.
◆ Ask pupils to make up a self-help card entitled 'A friend is ...'. Suggest they illustrate the card using cartoons and magazine cuttings.

Outcomes

◆ Knowledge and expression of the specific characteristics of friendship.
◆ Knowledge of the social skills of making and keeping good friends.
◆ Acknowledgement of and empathy with those who have difficulty making friends.

Friends for life?

1. List six things you can do to make friends.

1. _____
   _____
2. _____
   _____
3. _____
   _____
4. _____
   _____
5. _____
   _____
6. _____
   _____

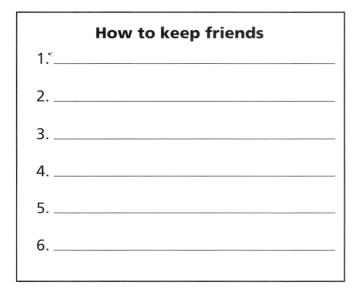

2. List six things you can do to keep your friends and six things to lose friends.

How to keep friends	**How to lose friends**
1. _____	1. _____
2. _____	2. _____
3. _____	3. _____
4. _____	4. _____
5. _____	5. _____
6. _____	6. _____

ACTIVITY BANK: *Coping with Change*

New friends, new interests?

What happens when I make new friends?

AIMS

To highlight how pupils will form new relationships and friendships in secondary school and may consequently need to revise their views of existing relationships and even their own identities.

Teaching Points

◆ At secondary school, pupils will make new friends who may introduce them to new interests that may not be shared by existing friends.
◆ Some pupils will need to cope with such changes, both in themselves and in their friends, and this may involve dealing with rejection and associated feelings and types of behaviour, such as a loss of self-esteem or a weakening of self-image.
◆ Adults within the school and home context will need to be particularly sensitive to such changes and attempt to provide pupils with appropriate support in dealing with any difficulties.
◆ It is good to make 'new' friends and important to value 'old' ones.

USING THE ACTIVITY SHEET

The focus of the activity is to explore how new friendships affect existing friendships and to equip pupils to identify and cope with any feelings of loss and rejection.

Step 1 Ask pupils to draw on their personal experience to list their answers to these questions individually: Do friends always have to share the same interests? Do friends have to share the same values? (You may need to explain 'values' as referring to belief systems such as religion, politics and so on.) What do we mean by a 'best' friend? Can someone have more than one 'best' friend? Invite responses from the class and write them on the board.

Step 2 Split the class into groups and ask them to describe three friendship problems and to suggest appropriate solutions. Give an example: 'Your best friend has started going to a tennis club and has become friendly with another boy or girl. They are going to watch a match next Wednesday. You have not been invited and feel jealous, but you still want to be friends.'

Step 3 Choose one problem and ask the group to act out the scenario to the class. Highlight problems and solutions in a class discussion.

Step 4 Ask pupils to complete the activity sheet.

Extension Activities

◆ Invite pupils to write a poem called 'Loneliness is …'. Ask them to think of words and phrases to describe how it feels to be lonely and rejected.
◆ Working with a partner, ask the pupils to make a list of 'Ten top tips – How to keep friends' (e.g. don't be jealous of their other friends; be loyal and don't chat behind their back). You could involve the ICT Department using suitable graphics.

Outcomes

◆ An understanding that friends can share different interests and values, which may change over time.
◆ Understanding the characteristics of a 'best' friend and the idea of 'sharing' friends.
◆ Acknowledging the importance of understanding and respecting the different value systems and beliefs of others.

New friends, new interests?

Penny's problem

My best friend has been a good friend since we were in the reception class at our primary school.

Since we have come to secondary school, she has become very religious and says she can't come around to my house to listen to CDs any more. She says God thinks that this music is bad.

She has changed so much and I don't know what to do. Can you help?

Penny

Yes! This is my advice

Paul's problem

My friend always liked playing football. We were both in the team at primary school and we went to matches with my uncle nearly every week.

Now he suddenly says he's not bothered any more as he has too much work to do for the Pupil Council. I feel left out, bored and lonely. Can you help?

Paul

Yes! This is my advice

The bully box

Respecting differences in others

AIMS

To highlight the fact that, although pupils may experience pressure to conform to their peer group's behaviour, it is perfectly acceptable to be different, and that bullying those who are different is wrong.

Teaching Points

◆ With the onset of puberty, physical and emotional changes run in parallel with a growing awareness of what is acceptable in the social context of the group, in terms of appearance, fashion, social groupings, interests and classroom image.

◆ Reinforce the idea that it is acceptable to be different but it is not acceptable to bully or tease those who do not want or feel able to conform to peer pressure.

USING THE ACTIVITY SHEET

The focus of the activity is to explore the pressures pupils may feel to conform to their peer group, and to make pupils aware of some of the causes of bullying.

Step 1 Discuss the concept of peer pressure using the following questions as prompts: What kind of things do young people sometimes feel under pressure to do? What are the pressures we all put on each other? What happens to those who do not conform or match up to the accepted picture of what they should be? How should we treat people who are, or want to be, different? Write initial responses and ideas on the board.

Step 2 Split the class into pairs. Ask each pair to make a list of eight pressures that a pupil might face. Ask pairs to join together and to jot down, in note form, what advice they would offer to that pupil to help deal with each specific pressure. Suggest an example, such as pressure to be thin, and solutions: diet; don't worry, it's only puppy fat and will go; exercise and so on.

Step 3 Invite the groups to report back the pressures and agreed solutions. Highlight any themes that become apparent, such as appearance, actions, behaviour and activities.

Step 4 Ask pupils to complete the activity sheet.

Extension Activities

◆ Work with the class to draw up a set of statements supporting the idea that 'Everyone is allowed to be different.'. They should think carefully about how people feel if they know that they do not 'fit in' – what can they do? Why can't they be themselves and not have to worry about what other people think?

◆ Ask pupils to think about the effects of bullying.

◆ The pupils could produce a list of actions that they think should be taken against a bully, recognising that the bully might need help.

Outcomes

◆ Recognising that it is possible to respond positively to peer pressure.

◆ Realising the importance of respecting other people and their differences.

◆ Recognising that bullies might need help.

The bully box

Miss West found these two letters in the bully box:

1. *'Please help me. I am being bullied because I am fat. I've tried to lose weight but I can't. Five girls in my class punch and kick me when the teacher's not looking. I can't stand it. Please help me. T'*

2. *'Help. I am being bullied by two boys because I have got good grades. They have not done as well as I have, but they could do if they tried. They say I'm a creep and a swot, and last week they punched me and took my money out of my bag. They now say I have to give them £5 a week or they won't stop. I'm scared. H'*

Pretend you are Miss West. Write responses to these two letters and try to solve the problems these two pupils are facing. Discuss your ideas with a friend.

Dear T	*Dear H*

What's happening to me?

Facing and coping with physical change

AIMS

To highlight the physical changes that students will experience with the onset of puberty and to develop practical ways of coping with these changes.

Teaching Points

◆ This sensitive topic should not be discussed until the pupils have settled into their new school and feel comfortable with the teacher and one another.
◆ It should be adapted, if necessary, to meet the requirements of the school's sex education policy.
◆ On transfer to secondary school, most pupils will have reached, or be approaching, the onset of puberty. The physical changes at this stage will be evident and will vary considerably.
◆ Emotional changes will run in parallel with these physical developments and both will require sensitive support from adults, both in school and at home.
◆ Reassure pupils that these changes are normal and ensure that they can understand and anticipate them. Use accurate information to counteract fears and myths.

USING THE ACTIVITY SHEET

The focus of the activity is to explore how the pupils experience physical changes, to ensure that they can make best use of available support structures and develop their own self-help strategies.

Step 1   Explain to the pupils that the purpose of the activity is to help them learn how to deal with physical changes.

Step 2   Ask the pupils to complete the first part of the activity sheet in which they compile a list of the physical changes that happen during adolescence.

Step 3   Ask the pupils, in pairs, to circle any of the changes they have listed that might cause problems for an adolescent. They then describe one problem on the 'postcard'.

Collect the 'postcards' and distribute them to other groups who write (on the reverse of them) possible ways to solve the problems.

Step 4   Ask the groups to separate their problem-and solution-postcards into two sets: those that the adolescent could sort out for himself or herself and those for which he or she needs help. Ask them to read out those from the second set. Where can they get the help they need and who can help them? On the board, list sources of help (within families, in the school and outside the school).

Extension Activities

◆ Ask pupils, in pairs, to act out a radio talk-show on teenage issues discussing coping with body change. They must take on the roles of a talk-show host and teenager.
◆ The pupils could compile a list of sources that can help with personal problems such as those they have identified. It should include the name of the teacher/s who they can approach.

Outcomes

◆ An awareness that, if problems are encountered, many other adolescents face similar problems, and awareness of sources of help.

What's happening to me?

1. List the physical reproductive changes that happen during adolescence.

_____

_____

_____

_____

_____

_____

_____

_____

_____

2. Circle any changes that might cause problems or embarrassment to an adolescent.

3. On the 'postcard' below, describe one problem or embarrassment that might happen.

Changing moods

Coping with emotional changes

— AIMS —

To highlight the emotional changes that students will experience alongside physical changes and to identify ways of coping with these sometimes difficult feelings.

Teaching Points

◆ Significant physical and emotional changes stem from the huge increase in hormonal activity that takes place during puberty.
◆ Many pupils will experience rapid changes in emotional states, over which they have little or no control. They may feel confused, not understanding what has prompted such strong reactions and mood swings.
◆ Teachers and parents need to recognise the difficulties teenagers are going through and provide secure environments in which problems can be sensitively handled. It is important that pupils recognise this as a 'normal' part of growing up.

— USING THE ACTIVITY SHEET —

The focus of the activity is to explore feelings that pupils frequently experience, to categorise them as either comfortable or uncomfortable and to identify ways of coping with uncomfortable feelings and situations.

Step 1 Ask pupils to suggest an alphabetical list of words for 'feelings' and 'emotions'. Write their responses on the board. Ask them to classify the feelings as 'comfortable' or 'uncomfortable'. Record these classifications on the board. Discuss which feelings might need to be controlled, when and how.

Step 2 Split the class into small groups. Ask each group to think of a situation in which someone might feel a strong, uncomfortable emotion (refer to the list on the board).

Ask each group to act out an appropriate scenario to the class. Ask the other groups to suggest ways of dealing with the situation. Focus on how it is possible to control some emotions and to avoid or cope better with uncomfortable situations.

Step 3 Ask pupils to complete the activity sheet.

Extension Activities

◆ Ask pupils to pretend that they are an agony aunt or uncle writing to Kelly, who feels like crying all the time and doesn't know why. Their letters could be published in the form of a magazine 'problem page'.
◆ Encourage pupils to develop a self-control strategy for anger, making a list of things that might make someone feel angry. Ask them to think about how they can show that they are angry without hitting or shouting. Invite them to write down their ideas for controlling anger.

Outcomes

◆ Developing personal responsibility for our emotions and empathy towards each other; learning to control anger and to distinguish between strong and mild feelings, and those that are comfortable and uncomfortable.
◆ Recognising that people cannot always understand why we feel the way we do – particularly during adolescence when hormones are extremely active. The best advice is not to panic!

Changing moods

Consider each feeling and write about a time when you felt like this. What did you do?
How did you react? Do you wish that you had reacted differently? What would you do now?

Angry

When I felt like this

_____

What I did

_____

I wish I had

_____

Now I would

_____

Embarrassed

When I felt like this

_____

What I did

_____

I wish I had

_____

Now I would

_____

Ashamed

When I felt like this

_____

What I did

_____

I wish I had

_____

Now I would

_____

Jealous

When I felt like this

_____

What I did

_____

I wish I had

_____

Now I would

_____

Different kinds of friendship

Getting used to new kinds of relationships

— AIMS —

To help pupils to understand and enjoy the different kinds of friendships they experience.

Teaching Points

◆ Pupils should be aware that they can have different friends for different purposes with whom they can enjoy different kinds of relationships.

◆ A major change for pupils at this stage will be their growing awareness of their own sexuality and that of others, and of the new and different types of relationships forming around them.

◆ The physical and emotional changes will not be easy for some pupils to cope with and neither will the associated changes in relationships.

◆ Pupils need opportunities to discuss these changes and to understand that they do not need to feel isolated, pressurised or uncomfortable about their changing feelings for their friends. Such changing relationships are a 'normal' part of growing up.

USING THE ACTIVITY SHEET

The focus of the activity is to consider the reasons why people have different friends with whom they spend time for different reasons and on different occasions.

Step 1   As an individual activity, ask the pupils to complete the activity sheet. Ask members of the class to read out their answers. Can the pupils explain why people do not spend all their spare time with the same friend?

Step 2   Split the class into groups and give each group a 'relationship problem', for example: 'My friend Hayley has gone to a football match with Clare. She didn't ask me if I wanted to go'; 'I went shopping for clothes with my sister. My friend Laura is not speaking to me because of it'; 'Jack has been playing computer games all afternoon with Bob. I hate computer games. I was hoping that Jack would come and play football with me' and 'Rosie is captain of the netball team. She didn't choose me to play and I'm her best friend.' They should describe the feelings of the people and explain why they acted as they did.

Step 3   Ask the pupils to devise solutions for the problems faced by each set of friends. Emphasise the importance of talking to their friends about these problems.

Extension Activities

◆ Ask the pupils to carry out a survey of the things people of different ages enjoy doing with their friends and to make a collage of different kinds of friendships and the things friends of different ages do together.

◆ The pupils could write the dialogue of an imaginary situation in which all their friends from different places meet. What would they say to one another?

Outcomes

◆ Acknowledgement of the value of self-help and mutual support at school, at home and among friends to solve problems caused by changes in relationships.

◆ An understanding of the value of talking through issues and working with friends to solve relationship problems.

Different kinds of friendship

1. On the friendship wheel, write the names of the friends you spend time with in each location. Think about why you do different things with different friends.

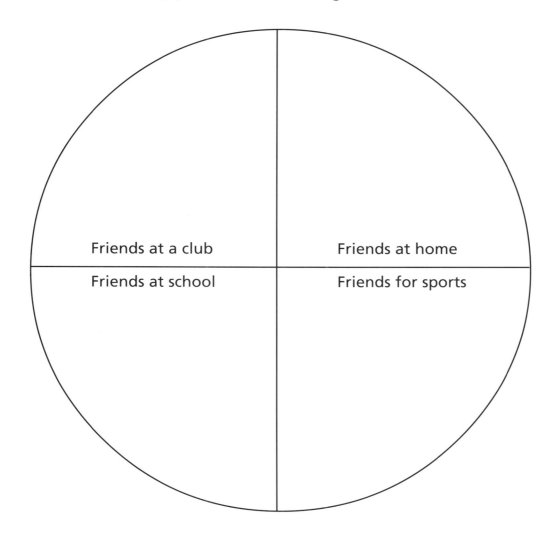

Friends at a club | Friends at home

Friends at school | Friends for sports

2. Make a chart that shows the activities you have enjoyed with friends during the past month.

Friend	Activities

ACTIVITY BANK: *Coping with Change*

Girlfriends and boyfriends

What do we want from different relationships?

AIMS

To highlight the differing notions of a 'girlfriend' and the pressures that girls in particular may feel at this stage with regard to sexual and emotional relationships.

Teaching Points

- There will be a considerable gap between the two gender groups in terms of physical and emotional development and girls will tend to appear more mature, both emotionally and physically.
- However, both sexes will have to cope with forming new friendships, losing existing friendships and the new 'value' placed upon having a friendship with a member of the opposite sex.
- Girls will probably experience more pressure to have a boyfriend and a sexual relationship at an earlier age than the boys in their peer group and will consequently need to develop ways of saying 'no'.
- Emphasise the importance of all pupils acting as a support for one another rather than putting added pressure on to each other to conform to some mythical norm.

USING THE ACTIVITY SHEET

The focus of the activity is to explore how pupils can cope with a range of problems and situations arising from personal relationships.

Step 1 Ask half the class to consider the following questions: What is your definition of a 'girlfriend'? What makes the best kind of 'girlfriend' for another girl? What makes the best kind of 'girlfriend' for a boy? Ask the other half of the class to consider the same questions in relation to boyfriends. They can then complete the appropriate sections of question 1 on the activity sheet.

Step 2 Split the class into groups in which half the members answered the first set of questions

and the other half answered the second set. The members of each group share their answers and identify any that occur in more than one section of the sheet. They list the characteristics that apply to all friendships (boy + boy, girl + girl and boy + girl) and those that apply only to mixed gender friendships.

Step 3 Ask the pupils to complete question 2 on the activity sheet.

Extension Activities

- The pupils could identify the problems that occur in mixed gender friendships (the ending of such friendships and forming of new ones and the physical attractions that are present that might lead to the pressure to have sex).
- Problems raised in the above activity can be written on to cards that the teacher can read out in class; the pupils can discuss the best ways to cope with these problems.

Outcomes

- An understanding of the similarity in the qualities of a good friendship and a good relationship.
- An understanding of the need for mutual support and empathy within the peer group to overcome problems experienced through relationship changes.

Girlfriends and boyfriends

1. Answer the questions allocated to your group.

What makes a good
female friend for a girl?

_____
_____
_____
_____
_____

What makes a good
male friend for a girl?

_____
_____
_____
_____
_____

What makes a good
male friend for a boy?

_____
_____
_____
_____
_____

What makes a good
female friend for a boy?

_____
_____
_____
_____
_____

2. Which characteristics from your group's lists describe all kinds of friendships?

_____
_____
_____
_____
_____

Family troubles

Coping with separation and divorce in the family

AIMS

To highlight the often traumatic changes and feelings that pupils may experience when parents or carers separate or divorce and the positive and constructive ways these feelings can be dealt with.

Teaching Points

Materials needed
A flipchart for the focus group work.

◆ This topic should be taught sensitively. Teachers should be aware of pupils who may be currently experiencing separation or divorce in the family. If possible, make additional support and counselling available to pupils both in and out of school.
◆ Many pupils will have knowledge or experience of changing adult relationships by this stage in their school careers, either on a personal level or through their peers.
◆ The growing awareness or the initial shock of learning that a family group may have to change is probably the most difficult problem for the children involved.
◆ There are complex 'normal' associated feelings such as rejection, anger, sadness and fear, all of which need to be dealt with in order to allow those involved to construct a more positive future.

USING THE ACTIVITY SHEET

The focus of the activity is to explore why relationships may break up and to encourage pupils to work together in order to give support and constructive advice to each other.

Step 1   Discuss with the class some of the problems faced by young people when parents or carers divorce. Record their responses on the board.

Step 2   Ask pupils to complete the activity sheet.

Step 3   Split the class into groups and ask each group to focus on the following problem: Tara's parents have decided to get a divorce. Her mum is moving back to Ireland and wants Tara to go with her and live in Dublin. Tara has just started secondary school and doesn't really want to leave now. She is desperately worried about her dad and doesn't want to leave him alone. What should she do? What advice do you give her? Ask pupils to write down their ideas.

Step 4   Focus on the similarities and differences in pupils' ideas and highlight the most logical or convincing advice they give. Collate responses on a flipchart.

Extension Activities

◆ Explain that 'rejection' is a word used to describe how people feel when someone has left them or apparently doesn't want to be near them any more. Ask pupils to think of how it must feel to experience rejection; invite them to jot down as many feelings as they can (e.g. anger, sadness, frustration).

Outcomes

◆ The development of empathy and respect for others.
◆ Clarification of pupils' own thoughts, feelings and opinions regarding divorce and separation.

Family troubles

Pat's parents have decided to split up. They seem to have argued for months and everyone in the family has felt very unhappy. Pat and his sister Jade now face a big change, as Dad will be moving out to a flat around the corner from their house. Think about how each member of the family must be feeling. What are they worried about? Write your responses in the speech bubbles.

Dad

I am worried about

Mum

I am worried about

Pat and Jade

We are worried about

A new family

Learning to live with new people in my life

AIMS

To highlight some of the difficulties that pupils may experience when their parents or carers form a new relationship and the ways in which they might cope best when entering or taking on a 'new family'.

Teaching Points

◆ As with Activities 14 and 16, this topic will need sensitive handling, according to the needs of the pupils.

◆ Many pupils will have either experienced for themselves or observed a friend going through the changes associated with their parents forming new relationships.

◆ With the increasing number of pupils whose parents choose not to live together, many will have had to become accustomed to making adjustments in terms of parents' new partners and their partner's children.

◆ Many pupils will have gained a 'new family' if and when parents remarry or form new relationships. This activity aims to highlight the necessary adjustments and changes, particularly for the pupils involved.

USING THE ACTIVITY SHEET

The focus of the activity is to explore the range of changes that might result from parents forming new relationships and to identify the associated feelings.

Step 1 Ask the class to identify the main changes that happen when their parents form new relationships. Issues may include money, new home, new siblings, new area, new school and so on. Ask them how they think the adults feel and what their motives and worries are. Ask them how the children feel and what problems they might have, particularly concerning relationships with new siblings and parents. Record their responses on the board.

Step 2 Split the class into small groups. Ask them to think of five changes that the children in the family might experience, the feelings associated with the change and the advice that they themselves would then give to members of their peer group experiencing such changes. Ask pupils to record their ideas in three columns headed 'change', 'feelings' and 'advice'.

Step 3 Invite feedback from the group activities. Highlight the most practical and sensible pieces of advice that the pupils have formulated.

Step 4 Ask pupils to complete the activity sheet.

Extension Activities

◆ Ask the class to look at the activity from another person's viewpoint. Ask them what Emma's letter would look like. What would she say about Trudi? Suggest they write her letter to the agony aunt or uncle and make up a response.

◆ Ask pupils to construct a 'List of self-help strategies – How to cope in a new family'; for example: 'Talk about how you feel.' 'Let everyone say what they need or want.' 'Set ground rules.'

Outcomes

◆ The development of skills of cooperation and empathy.

◆ An identification of the major feelings associated with this type of change and how to articulate these emotions and cope with them in practical ways.

A new family

Can you help Trudi solve this problem? Be an agony aunt or uncle and write a reply to her.

Dear Chris

Please can you help me? I'm so fed up and really unhappy. Last year my mum and dad split up. I stayed with Mum because she kept our house near school and Dad moved down to Southampton because his job changed.

It was bad but we got on OK, until she met Kevin. He has now moved in with us. He's not my dad, but he's OK. The problem is that his kids have come too. They are twins and a year older than me and I have to share my room with Emma . Joe is now in the box room.

The trouble is that she is so selfish. She has taken my stuff and wears my clothes without asking, plus she's stolen all the make-up that Nan gave me last Christmas. She plays her music really loudly and I can't do my homework. I've tried telling Mum but she doesn't seem interested. I feel like running away. No one is listening to me. Emma says I'm a spoiled brat and a creep for doing my homework. She was in trouble for not doing hers. Please help me.

Trudi

Dear Trudi

Losing a loved one

Helping ourselves and others when we lose someone we love

AIMS

To engender an understanding of what it means to be bereaved and to highlight associated issues of existence.

Teaching Points

◆ This topic should be taught with a sensitive approach. It may not be suitable for pupils who have recently experienced bereavement. If possible, make additional support and counselling available to pupils both in and out of school.

◆ Experiencing the changes brought about by a death in the family is a difficult and complex process.

◆ Experiences will vary widely but all pupils, at this stage, will benefit from gaining a further awareness and understanding of fundamental issues such as: Who am I? Where am I going? What does dying mean?

◆ Emphasise the universality of the feelings associated with the loss of a loved person and the types of support, both personal and professional, that are available to pupils.

◆ It is important for pupils to develop an awareness of how they can support each other in such difficult situations.

USING THE ACTIVITY SHEET

The focus of the activity is to explore the ways in which death affects us and our families.

Step 1 Discuss with the whole class the following questions: How do people behave when they are grieving? What kinds of things bring back memories of the people who have died? (e.g. hearing expressions they often used or songs they liked to hum or sing, seeing their empty chairs or coming across tangible things like their possessions, photographs of them or their handwriting.) Collate the pupils' responses on the board.

Step 2 Ask the pupils what people can do to cope with grief. Focus on positive ideas, such as remembering things that were special about the person (things he or she said or did, times enjoyed together), looking at things that bring back pleasant memories, such as photographs or tickets, programmes or souvenirs from special occasions, or even recalling things the person taught them or helped them with. Ask the pupils to complete the activity sheet.

Step 3 Invite the pupils to share some of their memories with the rest of the class. Do not collate their responses in any way (this would de-personalise them), just share them. Ask the pupils how this activity could help them to comfort someone who had lost a loved one. What would they say and do? What practical suggestions could they make that would help someone to treasure their memories of the dead person? Discuss also how soon it might be appropriate to try to help in this way — some people might want to be left alone for a while (perhaps just to cry) before they are ready, or want, to begin to cope with grief.

Extension Activities

◆ Suggest that pupils ask their parents about their great-grandparents and see if they can find any photos or information about them and things that belonged to them. Invite them to make an illustrated family tree showing the different generations in their family.

Outcomes

◆ An increased awareness of the different causes of death, the strong feelings associated with bereavement and the ways in which people can be helped through and out of bereavement and loss.

Losing a loved one

Think of someone you knew who has died. What made that person special? What will you always remember about him or her? Write at least ten things on the scroll.

Memories of _____

What do I believe?

What it means to follow a religion

AIMS

To highlight the variety of belief systems that exist and the need for pupils to respect alternative ways of living and believing.

Teaching Points

Materials needed
Reference material on a variety of world religions.

◆ Pupils will become more aware of the variety of belief systems that exist within and outside the school community. This may mean that, perhaps for the first time, they are presented with alternative ways of living and believing.

◆ It is extremely important to emphasise the changes that the adoption of a specific religion or set of beliefs will bring, alongside the importance of respecting different value systems and beliefs.

USING THE ACTIVITY SHEET

The focus of the activity is to explore the 'myths' that pupils may hold about other people's religious beliefs.

Step 1 Discuss with the class the following questions: What does it mean to 'have a religion'? What is the difference between having a religion and having a set of moral beliefs? Write the answers in two columns on the board.

Step 2 Split the class into small groups. Ask each group to list three myths (that is, people's unfounded beliefs about different religions), such as: 'Muslim women have no rights and are treated like servants.' Ask groups to swap their lists around.

Step 3 Provide reference material (or the pupils could use the school library) in which the facts can be checked. Now ask the groups to

respond to each 'myth' with a 'reality' such as: 'Muslim women have many rights, including owning property, and they are encouraged to educate themselves.'

Step 4 Discuss the results of the group activity. Focus on the way in which many of these myths are accepted by people who have a different religion or belief system and how, consequently, it is vital to search for the realities in order to dispel and diffuse ignorant and racist perspectives. Emphasise the importance of tolerance and living together peacefully.

Step 5 Ask pupils to complete the activity sheet.

Extension Activities

◆ Ask pupils to work with a partner and interview each other about their religion for three minutes. They should think of at least four questions to ask and agree these together. Invite them to rehearse their scene and then perform it to the rest of the class.

◆ Invite the class to draw up a joint statement about the importance of mutual understanding of and respect for people's beliefs.

Outcomes

◆ Recognising that we need to respect each others' beliefs and people's rights to hold those particular beliefs.

◆ Appreciating some of the reasons for intolerance of others' beliefs, such as fear and misunderstanding.

◆ Identifying a personal belief system.

◆ Distinguishing between myths and facts.

What do I believe?

Think carefully about what you believe. What are your beliefs and moral values?
Make up a charter of ten beliefs.

My beliefs

1. I believe _____
   _____
   _____

2. I believe _____
   _____
   _____

3. I believe _____
   _____
   _____

4. I believe _____
   _____
   _____

5. I believe _____
   _____
   _____

6. I believe _____
   _____
   _____

7. I believe _____
   _____
   _____

8. I believe _____
   _____
   _____

9. I believe _____
   _____
   _____

10. I believe _____
    _____
    _____

Vote for me!

Understanding and developing one's own political views

— AIMS —

To highlight the variety of political views that exist and how they affect and shape our everyday lives.

Teaching Points

◆ Pupils need to develop their awareness of a variety of political views and the ways in which these influence, change and shape their everyday lives.

◆ For some pupils, secondary school will be one of many environments that will present them with differing views, belief systems and political standpoints.

◆ Many pupils will have been exposed to information about political groups and their parties through the media and perhaps through family conversation and debates. However, some may have had fewer opportunities to formulate their own feelings and views.

◆ This session will aim to provide pupils with an opportunity to consider the various political options and to gain a further insight into each other's perspectives.

— USING THE ACTIVITY SHEET —

The focus of the activity is to enable pupils to gain an insight into how they might become part of a political system that may or may not be able to effect change.

Step 1 Initiate a class discussion, focusing on the questions: What do we mean by 'politics'? What are the main political parties in this country and what belief systems do they represent? How are political beliefs different from religious beliefs? Write the responses in three columns on the board.

Step 2 Split the class into groups. Ask each group to pretend it is a political party and to formulate a campaign with 'Five reasons why you should vote for us.'. Ask them to focus on the changes they would like to try and bring about, such as 'More money for schools so that ...', 'More hospitals so that ...' and so on.

Step 3 Ask pupils to complete the activity sheet.

Step 4 Invite feedback from the group activity. The pupils might like to nominate one student to take on this task or present the ideas as a group, in the style of a party political broadcast. Once each group has presented its views, ask the class to vote for one of the parties and highlight why any one group may have been more convincing or popular than another.

Extension Activities

◆ Ask pupils to make a list of ten characteristics of a good citizen and to compare their list with that of a friend. What do they agree about? Where do they disagree? Why do they think this is so?

◆ Explain that, in some countries, people are put into prison because of their beliefs. Ask the class to research some specific examples; an organisation like Amnesty International might be of help.

Outcomes

◆ The development and expression of pupils' own political views and awareness of their individual right to have these views and values.

◆ An identification of what makes a good citizen and the importance of tolerance and respect for others' views.

Vote for me!

If you were a politician you would need to persuade people to vote for you. Imagine that you are standing for Parliament. What would you say? What changes would you want to implement? Draw up your own personal manifesto, giving reasons why people should vote for you. Illustrate it with a self-portrait.

Dear Voter

Your candidate: _____

You should vote for me because:

_____

_____

_____

_____

_____

_____

_____

_____

_____

_____

_____

_____

_____

_____

_____

No work for some

How unemployment affects individuals and families

AIMS

To highlight the effect of unemployment upon families and individuals and the stigmas that may be attached to those involved.

Teaching Points

- Pupils need to be able to see things from another perspective and understand how everyone, at certain times in their lives, can be affected by economic change.
- Some pupils will have personal experience of unemployment in their own family and the resulting financial constraints and changes to lifestyle. Others may be aware of the difficulties experienced by adults around them.
- Most pupils and their families will probably experience economic change as a direct result of unemployment at some time in their lives.
- It is consequently particularly important to raise awareness of the associated problems, discuss any stigmas attached to such a change and highlight the available support structures.

USING THE ACTIVITY SHEET

The focus of the activity is to explore the main problems and changes associated with unemployment and to dispel some of the myths associated with being 'on benefit'.

Step 1 Split the class into pairs and ask them to discuss and write down their answers to the following questions: What are the main problems facing an unemployed person? Why do some people find it harder to get or keep a job than others? How can unemployed people help themselves and each other? Write responses on the board, handling them with sensitivity. Highlight the extent to which unemployment is a 'political issue' and a 'social problem'.

Step 2 Split the class into groups and ask them to list five myths and realities regarding

unemployment; for example, myth: 'Unemployed people do not want to work and are lazy.'; Reality: 'Most people are not lazy and would like the opportunity to work.'.

Step 3 Ask each group to nominate one person to report back to the rest of the class. Discuss where and why these myths were created and why it is important to identify the realities in order to dispel ignorant and inaccurate perspectives.

Step 4 Ask pupils to complete the activity sheet.

Extension Activities

- Ask pupils to imagine that they are unemployed and that they have been trying to find work for a year. Ask them to think about their attempts to find work and what happened, and to write about it in the form of a diary.
- Ask the class to research and compile an advice sheet on how to help unemployed people, including where they could go for help and how they could help themselves.

Outcomes

- An understanding of the social problems associated with unemployment, the support available and a development of the ability to see a situation or problem from another person's perspective.
- An understanding of why some individuals or groups can be intolerant or lacking in understanding of the problems faced by unemployed people.

No work for some

Toby

Yasmin

Lucy

My dad lost his job in the mines eight years ago. We have never had a holiday. My friend has asked me to go with her to Spain, but there isn't any money. What can I do? Toby.

I lost my job last week. Now I'm not going to have enough money to buy the kids the new trainers and clothes they want. I feel so sad about it. We're going to have to be very careful with money from now on. What can I do? Yasmin.

My twelve-year-old sister is so selfish. Dad hasn't got much money. He's on benefit and hasn't worked for three years, but she keeps on and on about wanting make-up and clothes and money for going out. It upsets him. What can I do? Lucy.

What advice would you give? What do you think these people are feeling? Are they 'right' to feel this way? Complete the three replies on the correspondence cards.

Dear Toby
I think

Dear Yasmin
I think

Dear Lucy
I think

Peer pressure

Being the person I want to be

AIMS

To highlight how peer pressure changes over time and requires a variety of responses.

Teaching Points

◆ Peer pressure appears to affect most pupils at some time during their school careers.

◆ Being different from the norm can cause enormous difficulties for some, while others relish any opportunity to stand out from the crowd. However, knowing what is acceptable within the social context of particular groups will be a real concern for many pupils.

◆ Initially, peer pressure may involve activities, hobbies and friendships, but can change to include more serious moral and emotional dilemmas, including pressure to have sex, to smoke or take drugs, or to adopt certain extreme belief systems.

◆ This session aims to encourage pupils to develop responses and self-help strategies to deal with a variety of pressures.

USING THE ACTIVITY SHEET

The focus of the activity is to explore how pupils can 'best' respond to peer pressure and to distinguish how these pressures can change over time.

Step 1   Ask pupils to discuss, in pairs, the following questions: What is 'peer pressure'? What sort of pressures do pupils feel now? How are these different from the pressures they felt last year? Write responses on the board.

Step 2   Split the class into groups to discuss five pressures that they feel they experienced last year and whether these pressures remain the same or have changed. Groups can record responses on a sheet of paper.

Step 3   Pin up responses from the group activity around the room and ask groups to nominate someone to report back their ideas. Highlight any agreements or disagreements regarding peer pressure experienced last year and this year and attempt to reach consensus as to the extent of the changes pupils have experienced in this time.

Step 4   Discuss the problem of the desire to give in to peer pressure and invite pupils to suggest ways to overcome this.

Step 5   Ask pupils to complete the activity sheet.

Extension Activities

◆ Invite pupils to think about how the media present the 'ideal' person. Ask them to make a list of ideal factors and then to consider what they think is ideal for themselves. Is there a difference?

◆ In groups, the pupils could enact a chat show entitled 'Teenage pressures – How to cope.'. They should take on the roles of pupils, host, teacher and parent, presenting everyone's differing views. Can they agree solutions?

Outcomes

◆ An understanding of what is meant by peer pressure and how to address its related problems.

◆ An articulation of pupils' own thoughts and feelings about peer pressure.

◆ An understanding that people can experience different kinds of peer pressure at different stages in their lives.

◆ A reinforcement of everyone's 'right' to be themselves, as long as this does not harm anyone else.

Peer pressures

Think of a problem relating to each issue. What is the pressure? What can you do in order to cope with it?

drugs

The problem _____

_____

The pressure _____

_____

The solution _____

_____

sex

The problem _____

_____

The pressure _____

_____

The solution _____

_____

diet

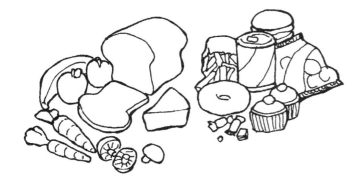

The problem _____

_____

The pressure _____

_____

The solution _____

_____

clothes

The problem _____

_____

The pressure _____

_____

The solution _____

_____

ACTIVITY BANK: *Coping with Change*

Changing roles

The roles I play and how others see me

AIMS

To highlight the variety of roles that people adopt and the ways in which these change through time and in different contexts.

Teaching Points

◆ Alongside the physical and emotional changes occurring at the onset of puberty, pupils will also experience a greater awareness and understanding of others around them and the different roles that they perform in their lives.

◆ They will gradually develop more empathy and an increased ability to understand perspectives and belief systems other than their own.

◆ Pupils will also become more aware of the different roles they are required to play, such as brother, sister, student, son, daughter, friend, girlfriend, boyfriend and so on, and the variety of skills they need to acquire in order to be successful in the process.

USING THE ACTIVITY SHEET

The focus of the activity is to explore and define a variety of roles and assess which is most appropriate to adopt in a given situation.

Step 1   Initiate a class discussion focusing on the following questions: What do we mean by a 'role'(for instance as a brother, sister or friend)? What are the roles that pupils might take on? Between which roles might disagreements and conflicts arise? Write responses in three columns on the board.

Step 2   Split the class into groups and ask each group to think of a 'role conflict scene', such as conflicts between parents and friends over going out or over clothes. Ask each group to focus on one problem, listing as many solutions as possible and finally devising an agreed best plan.

Step 3   Invite groups to report back to the rest of the class. Highlight areas of conflict, particularly those where pupils are seen to fill different roles by different people in their lives. Focus on the solutions that appear to be the most appropriate and sensible and will consequently be of most use in resolving the conflict.

Step 4   Ask the pupils to complete the activity sheet. Examples of areas where they might change their role include clothes, behaviour and the language they use. Examples of areas where they might stay the same would be beliefs, likes and dislikes.

Extension Activities

◆ Ask pupils to think about whom they admire most. What makes them admire that person? Ask them to make a list of the person's characteristics on a card, then swap their card with a friend and see if they can guess each other's role model.

◆ Invite everyone to make a list of all the different roles they perform. What are the difficulties and what are the possible solutions to the differences between them?

Outcomes

◆ Understanding the idea of taking on roles which may change and develop through time.

◆ Developing self-awareness, empathy and problem-solving skills.

Changing roles

1. Draw a self-portrait, or use a recent photo of yourself. In the clouds, write in the box your different roles in life at the moment. For example, you might be a pupil, a son, a baby-sitter, a boyfriend, a friend, and lots of other things.

2. On the other lines, write how you change in each role.
3. Think about the things that stay the same and write these below.

_____

_____

All change!

What have I learned from the changes in my life?

AIMS

To review the changes experienced by pupils; to what extent they have conformed to various pressures and to what extent they have developed ways of coping with changes and pressures.

Teaching Points

◆ This lesson is intended to review the series of lessons, providing pupils with the opportunity to examine changes both past and in progress, and to focus on the development of self-help strategies.
◆ Pupils have identified major physical changes alongside changes in their roles, responsibilities and relationships. They have had the opportunity to develop empathy with others and understanding of their views, and have begun to articulate their own beliefs.
◆ These lessons have also highlighted the pressures to conform from sources such as the peer group, the media, parents, families, schools and particularly adults in the community, and have also developed appropriate ways and means of coping with these pressures.

USING THE ACTIVITY SHEET

The focus of the activity is to explore how changes have affected both individuals and groups, and to highlight the support strategies available to pupils.

Step 1   Discuss with the class the main changes they have experienced at secondary school, both as individuals and as a group, and how the attitudes of others towards them have changed over this period. Write responses on the board.

Step 2   Split the class into groups. Ask them to focus on changes in one of the following categories: physical and emotional development; peer pressure and friendships; responsibility and roles; family and relationships; belief systems. Ask the group to list the main

changes in each category and then to identify the various support systems available to pupils experiencing such changes.

Step 3   Ask each group to nominate one person to report back to the rest of the class. Reinforce the available support systems and emphasise the importance of developing techniques and personal strategies to deal with change.

Step 4   Ask pupils to complete the activity sheet.

Extension Activities

◆ Ask pupils to work with a friend and remember how it felt to be a new pupil about to start secondary school. Ask them to write a letter to an imaginary pupil telling them about the changes they will experience and advising them on how best to cope.
◆ Ask pupils to think of three people they know quite well. Then ask them to think about any changes these people may have experienced. How do these changes compare to the ones the pupils have made recently?

Outcomes

◆ A recognition that everyone experiences change and that pupils can help themselves and others to cope with and learn from change.
◆ A reinforcement of the importance of empathising with others and respecting different beliefs and value systems.

All change!

Think and write about the changes you have experienced since starting secondary school.

Things that have changed	How they have changed
1. My appearance.	1.
2. My beliefs.	2.
3. My work.	3.
4. My friends.	4.
5. Pressures from friends and family.	5.
6. My ability to say 'no'.	6.
7. My roles and responsibilities.	7.
8. My hobbies and interests.	8.

Skills matrix

ACTIVITY/ SKILL	1	2	3	4	5	6	7	8	9	10	11	12	13	14	15	16	17	18	19	20	21	22
Analysing/Interpreting	●	●	●	●	●	●	●	●	●	●	●	●	●	●	●	●	●	●	●	●	●	●
Asserting				●	●	●												●		●	●	
Awareness	●	●	●	●	●	●	●	●	●	●	●	●	●	●	●	●	●	●	●	●	●	●
Collating			●	●	●	●			●	●			●				●				●	
Communicating	●	●	●	●	●	●	●		●	●	●	●	●	●	●	●	●	●	●	●	●	●
Comparing	●	●	●	●		●		●			●		●	●			●	●	●	●	●	●
Cooperating	●	●	●	●	●	●	●	●	●	●	●	●	●	●	●	●	●	●	●	●	●	●
Debating and discussing	●	●	●	●	●	●	●	●	●	●	●	●	●	●	●	●	●	●	●	●	●	●
Decision making	●	●	●	●	●	●					●		●	●				●		●		
Empathising	●	●	●		●	●	●	●	●	●	●	●	●	●	●	●	●		●	●	●	●
Evaluating	●	●	●	●	●	●	●	●	●	●	●	●	●	●	●	●	●	●	●	●	●	
Expressing (e.g. of beliefs, ideas and opinions)	●			●	●	●	●	●	●		●	●	●	●	●	●	●	●	●	●		
ICT		●						●														
Identity and self-esteem		●	●		●	●	●	●	●	●	●	●	●			●	●	●		●	●	●
Imagining		●	●	●	●	●		●		●		●		●		●			●	●		●
Investigating										●		●				●		●	●	●		
Knowledge	●	●	●	●	●		●		●	●			●	●		●	●	●		●		
Listening	●	●	●	●	●	●	●		●	●	●	●	●	●	●	●	●	●	●	●	●	●
Negotiating				●	●												●					
Perceiving			●		●	●		●	●	●		●	●	●	●		●	●	●	●	●	
Presenting		●	●													●	●	●		●		
Prioritising				●	●	●							●									
Problem solving	●	●	●	●	●	●	●		●	●	●	●	●	●	●	●			●	●	●	●
Respect				●	●	●		●	●	●	●	●	●	●		●	●	●		●		●
Responsibility	●	●	●	●	●	●	●		●	●	●	●	●	●				●	●	●	●	●
Understanding	●	●	●	●	●	●	●	●	●	●	●	●	●	●	●	●	●	●	●	●	●	●